FOUNTAINS ABBEY & STUDLEY ROYAL

North Yorkshire

The National Trust

The text on Fountains Abbey has been written by Mary Mauchline, that on Studley Royal by Lydia Greeves.

Lydia Greeves is particularly grateful to Mr W. T. C. Walker for his work on Studley Royal.

© 1988 The National Trust
Registered charity no. 205846
Reprinted 1995, 2000, 2002, 2003 (twice), 2007, 2008
revised 1989, 1993, 1998, 2004, 2005

ISBN 978-1-84359-123-8

Photographs: Matthew Antrobus pages 41, 54, 56, back cover; Bibliothèque Nationale, Dijon page 13; National Trust Photographic Library/Oliver Benn front cover; Andrew Butler page 64 (bottom); Dominic Cooper pages 4, 40; Martin Dohrn pages 8 (above), 29 (above), 60 (left); Chris Hayes page 52 (left); Mary Mauchline page 10; Charlie Waite pages 7, 8 (below), 35 (below right), 42, 53 (left), 55 (right), 57 (top left), 58 (above); Tony Whittaker pages 1, 39; C. H. Wood (Bradford) Ltd page 11; Geoffrey Wright pages 3, 5, 34, 43, 46, 47, 52 (right), 57 (top right), 58 (below), 59; Paul Harris page 64 (top). All other photographs are by Mike Williams. All photographs are the copyright of the National Trust with the exception of those on pages 10, 11 and 13.

The plan of the abbey on page 20–1 appears by courtesy of English Heritage.

Designed by James Shurmer

Phototypeset in Monotype Plantin Light Series 113 by Intraspan Ltd, Smallfield, Surrey (IS354)

Colour reproduction by Acculith 76, Barnet, Hertfordshire

Printed by Heanorgate for National Trust (Enterprises) Ltd Heelis, Kemble Drive, Swindon, Wilts SN2 2NA on stock made from 75% recycled fibre

(*Right*) The Temple of Fame, Studley Royal, on the high path along the top of the valley

CONTENTS

INTRODUCTION

A visit to Fountains Abbey and Studley Royal is a unique experience. No other site in Europe contains such a rich variety of monuments from past ages, together giving an unparalleled opportunity to appreciate the range of England's heritage. The wooded valley of the River Skell shelters not only the extensive ruins of Fountains Abbey itself, an outstanding example of the power of medieval monasticism, but also John Aislabie's early 18th-century water garden, adorned with Classical temples and statues, and the honey-coloured elegance of Fountains Hall, its beautiful late 16th-century facade epitomising the confidence of the age. In the deer park beyond the garden lies St Mary's Church, an essay in High Victorian Gothic and the religious masterpiece of the architect William Burges, its florid decoration a striking contrast to the Cistercian simplicity of Fountains. Each of these features is a superb example of its kind.

The text that follows includes suggested tours of the abbey (p.22) and garden (p.50). A complete tour of the garden (but not including a tour of the abbey or Seven Bridges Walk) takes about 2 hours, the medium route about $1\frac{3}{4}$ hours and the short walk about 45 minutes.

(*Right*) The dramatic valley of the lower Skell, where the river flows down a narrow gorge beside the park.

(*Left*) William Aislabie's surprise view in winter.

FOUNTAINS ABBEY

The North of England has a long tradition of monasticism. In Yorkshire, abbeys were established as early as the 7th century. In spite of the Danish invasions and settlement in the 9th and 10th centuries, the legacy of a golden age of monastic culture remained.

This enabled monasticism to revive quickly and effectively after the Norman Conquest in 1066. William I punished his rebellious Yorkshire subjects and then settled his followers on the forfeited lands. The Norman nobility, who were to become benefactors of Fountains Abbey, were enthusiastic patrons of the religious Orders in general. Benedictine abbeys like Whitby were restored and the Benedictine house of St Mary's, York, was founded in 1088–89 by monks from Whitby.

(*Right*) This view of the abbey shows how it is hidden away in the steep-sided valley. From a distance, only the top of the tower is visible.

(*Left*) The stone from which the abbey was built was hewn from the outcrops on the north (right-hand) side of the valley.

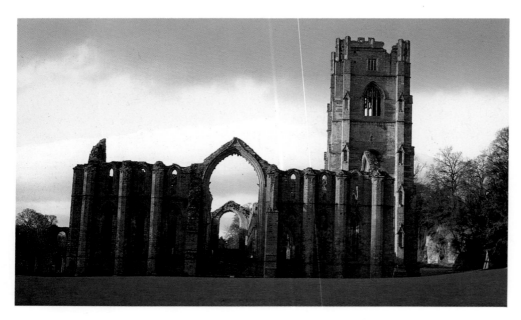

(*Above*) Fountains Abbey, the great east window in the Chapel of the Nine Altars echoed by the window over the west door.

(*Right*) The abbey reflected in the clear waters of the Skell. In monastic times the river would probably have been clouded with refuse.

These two stone carvings are now displayed in the little museum on the west side of abbey green: (*left*) St Mark, the Evangelist, writing his Gospel; his symbol, the winged lion of Resurrection, is at his feet; (*right*) the Annunciation; the Archangel Gabriel is holding a scroll bearing the words of his salutation.

A dispute at St Mary's led to the founding of Fountains Abbey. In the summer of 1132 a draft programme for the radical reform of St Mary's was presented to the elderly abbot by the leader of the dissident monks, Prior Richard. The reformers pleaded for a return to the basic principles of the early 6th-century Rule of St Benedict, humbly seeking God in worship, prayer and meditation, and interpreting literally the periods of manual work specified in the Rule. The relaxed atmosphere of their Benedictine abbey contrasted sharply with the disciplined attitude of the monks of the young Cistercian Order who had passed through the city that spring, 'rejoicing in their poverty', on their way to found Rievaulx Abbey as a daughter house of St Bernard's Cistercian abbey of Clairvaux in France.

Tension at St Mary's increased and Thurstan, Archbishop of York, intervened on behalf of the reformers, who included the five leading officials of the monastery. After a riot at the abbey in October 1132 he took the 13 monks, now exiled from their house, into his protection. They spent Christmas at his palace in Ripon and from there, on 27 December, the monks made their way three miles up the valley of the little River Skell to the site Thurstan had given them, together with some land for their sustenance.

Although described as a place 'more fit for wild beasts than men to inhabit', Skelldale was the veritable 'desert in the north' these men craved, a miniature ravine, rocky, overgrown, damp and desolate, where they might live like hermits seeking their souls' salvation. All the essential materials were there for the creation of the monastery: shelter from the rough northern weather, stone and timber for building, and an abundance of water from the Skell and the springs on the steep banks above. The abbey's name, St Mary of Fountains, may derive from these springs, but it has also been suggested that Fountains took its name from its guiding spirit, St Bernard de Fontaines, more familiarly known as Bernard of Clairvaux. All Cistercian abbeys were dedicated to the Virgin Mary.

Thurstan confirmed the election of Prior Richard as the first Abbot. But despite its spiritual zeal and physical endurance the community was not viable and it began to prove impossible for it to continue. In their despair, in 1133 the monks turned to Bernard of Clairvaux and the Cistercian Order for help.

The Cistercian Order had been founded in 1098 in France in circumstances very similar to Fountains and with the same ideals. The parent abbey of Citeaux, too, had begun with an exodus of monks, in this case to the swamps of Burgundy where,

One of the springs which may have given the abbey its name, St Mary of Fountains.

This aerial view of
Fountains Abbey shows
how the buildings are
clustered round the
cloister at the heart of the
monastery.

after appalling initial hardship, they had survived to found an Order. Apart from its compelling spiritual magnetism, the strength of Cistercianism lay in its constitution which provided for a close family relationship between mother and daughter houses. Unity was also fostered by an annual General Chapter every autumn at Citeaux, which all the abbots were obliged to attend and whose decisions were binding. Every Cistercian house conformed to the same customs but the masterstroke was the insistence on the identical layout of the buildings. Wherever he went, the Cistercian monk always felt at home.

It was St Bernard who gave the movement its early direction and crusading fervour. He became Abbot of Clairvaux, the third daughter house of Citeaux, in 1115 aged 25 and, until his death in 1153, made the Order a leading power in the affairs of Europe. His aim was to create an empire of Cistercian abbeys to fight for papal supremacy against the interference of secular rulers in ecclesiastical matters.

The chapter house arcade on the east side of the cloister.

To the monks in the Skell valley, membership of this now highly organised and forceful French Order, directly under papal control, seemed a betrayal of their ideals. Yet the loss of their independence was necessary if the community was to survive. In the autumn of 1135 the abbey was considered sufficiently secure and stable to be admitted into the Cistercian Order.

The rigour of the monks' daily life continued as before. They were forbidden to have underwear and were given the regulation habit of coarse undyed sheep's wool which had earned the Cistercians the name 'White Monks'. Breeches were provided for a journey, but when a monk returned they had to be washed and put back into the common stock. Woollen or cloth stockings and leather boots were worn. They had to familiarise themselves with the Cistercian language of gesture, since only in this way could communication be maintained in an Order committed to long periods of silence. The diet was barely above subsistence level. The monks of Fountains were as they had always been, 'poor as the poor of Christ'. As the years went by, these restrictions were relaxed or ceased to be practised through default or

This capital comes from a manuscript illuminated at Citeaux in the early 12th century. It is unusual in that it portrays everyday activities. Here two monks chop wood.

decree. Nevertheless the Cistercian Order has always been associated with the qualities of austerity and simplicity.

The same values held good in Cistercian architecture, a severe, unadorned style relying for impact and effect on mass and proportion, light and shade. There was a total rejection of extravagant decoration and applied ornament, which Bernard abhorred. Such self-expression mocked the beauty of God's creation, the results distracted the monks from their devotions and the cost was shameful. On the altar of a Cistercian church only a cross of painted wood and a candlestick of iron were permitted.

The ideals and aims of the Order are reflected in the efficient design of its buildings, which were planned to allow the monks to devote as much time as possible to their vocation. A mind fixed on the hope of achieving mystical communion with God and a life lived according to the example of Christ wasted neither time nor space on the things of this temporary world. Until the service of Compline in the evening, seven Offices (services) punctuated the day with periods for work, reading and meals. Whatever the monks were doing, words of prayer were constantly on their lips. Each room at Fountains had its purpose in God's workshop and was placed with regard both to religious symbolism and economy of organisation.

The most important development for the abbey was the introduction of the Cistercian system of lay brothers. They relieved the monks from the routine jobs of the abbey and worked its estates so that the monks might give themselves unreservedly to their life of prayer and meditation. These men, who were usually illiterate, were an integral part of a Cistercian house, taking monastic vows and having their own refectory, dormitory and infirmary within the monastery; hence the vast scale of abbeys of this Order. They shared the church, but were cut off from the 'choir' monks (so-called to distinguish them from the lay brothers) by screens that enclosed the west end of the nave, where they had their own altar. They attended fewer services, had longer hours of sleep and ate more plentifully, for they were the labour force of the house.

Without the lay brothers, Fountains could never have attained its great wealth or economic importance. Many served the abbey as masons, tanners, shoemakers and smiths, or in brewing or baking. But their chief role was to look after the abbey's vast flocks of sheep, which were carried on huge estates stretching westwards from Fountains into the Lake District and northwards to Teeside. By the middle of the 13th century Fountains was one of the richest religious houses in England. Although wool was the main source of its wealth, attracting buyers from Flanders

(*Right*) The undercroft to the monks' dormitory. The wall of the south transept beyond shows how the roof line of the dormitory cut across the original window openings when the abbey was enlarged in the second half of the 12th century.

and Italy, the abbey was also deeply involved in mining lead and working iron, quarrying stone, cattle rearing, horse breeding and other industrial and agricultural concerns.

The seeds of failure lay in the very success of this system. The presence of the lay brothers encouraged the monks to extend their estates far beyond what was necessary for monastic self-sufficiency and beyond what they could reasonably control effectively. The radiant idealism of the first generation was lost and the spiritual life of the abbey was eroded. Grandiose building projects based on unrealistic assessments of future income resulted in massive debts.

Economic collapse came in the 14th century when bad harvests, Scots raids and the Black Death exacerbated the effects of financial mismanagement. With papal permission, many monastic granges formerly controlled directly from the abbey were leased out to tenant farmers. For the rest of the abbey's life the monks tended to live on their rents with a mixed agrarian economy on those granges they still controlled directly. Dairy farming began to take the place of sheep farming by the late 15th century, especially on the granges in Nidderdale. With lay brothers no longer joining the community, the abbey was now forced to sell some of its other land and recruit a new community of servants at the abbey itself.

However, Fountains remained of considerable importance within the Cistercian Order and her abbots sat in Parliament. The abbacy of Marmaduke Huby (1495–1526) was a heartening period of revival. He represented the Cistercian Order in England and instigated a programme of reform. The number of monks at Fountains rose to 52; the more usual complement was about 30. The great Perpendicular tower built by Huby symbolises his hope for the abbey's future and his own initials boldly carved there, as elsewhere, spell out his ambition. Fountains was once again a flourishing concern with a fortune based on land, minerals and a treasury of plate and jewels, when the life of the abbey was brought abruptly to an end by the Dissolution of the Monasteries. Henry VIII's disagreement with the Pope over the annulment of his marriage, coupled with his need for money, convinced him of the wisdom of removing the influence of a foreign power from his country. England's great abbeys, owing allegiance to the Papacy, were a threat to his autocratic government.

Dissolution came in 1539, when the deed of surrender was signed in the chapter house. The Abbot, Marmaduke Bradley, who had served Henry VIII's commissioners very well, was rewarded handsomely. His pension was £100 a year, his prior's £8. Thirty monks received sums of about £6 each, the customary stipend for a country priest.

(*Right*) Details on the tower: (*above*) a niche on the east side of the tower is guarded by an angel holding a shield engraved with three horseshoes, an heraldic symbol associated with the abbacy of Marmaduke Huby; (*below*) a grotesque creature to the left of the lowest window on the east side of the tower; (*right*) the northern buttress on the east face of the tower, showing three of the four niches. These were never filled with statuary. Part of the inscription Abbot Huby carved on each side of his tower can be seen on the left

In 1540, the abbey buildings and over 200 hectares (500 acres) of land were sold by the Crown to Sir Richard Gresham, a merchant. They were then resold by a descendant, William Gresham of Itwood, to Stephen Proctor, who built Fountains Hall between 1598 and 1604, partly with stone from the abbey ruins.

Fountains Hall has a mellow, romantic quality. It is a perfect example of its period, bold and confident, built for peace and prosperity, not for defence. It shows similarities to the great Elizabethan architect Robert Smythson, who built Hardwick Hall in Derbyshire and Burton Agnes in Yorkshire. The exterior with its fashionable Renaissance details is a façade, concealing a great hall and upper chamber with kitchens below. A musicians' gallery is set across the building with a passage to the stairs underneath.

Sir Stephen was one of the new men, a Protestant, out to found a family and destroy the old Roman Catholic families of the area, the Mallories, the Yorkes and the Ingilbys. Upstairs in the Great Chamber of the Hall, the heraldic glass in the oriel window reflects his pretensions to gentility. James I knighted Proctor and used him to hunt down local adherents of the Old Faith. After his death in 1619, the Hall passed through several hands until the Roman Catholic Messenger family sold it in 1768 to William Aislabie, together with the abbey ruins which they had protected so reverently.

Fountains Hall, the expanse of glass recalling Hardwick Hall in Derbyshire.

(*Above*) The chimneypiece in the Great Chamber of
Fountains Hall, showing the stone carving of the
Judgement of Solomon.

(*Right*) The entrance to Fountains Hall, flanked by
Classical columns and martial figures.

PLAN OF
FOUNTAINS ABBEY

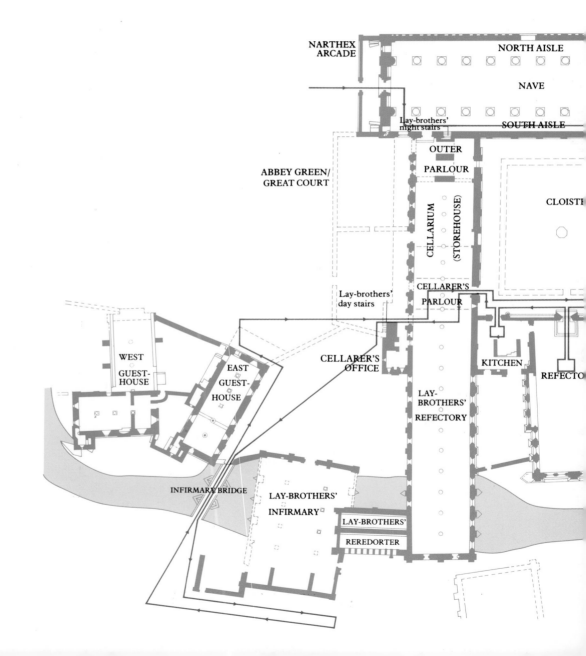

NARTHEX
ARCADE

NORTH AISLE

NAVE

Lay-brothers'
night stairs

SOUTH AISLE

OUTER

PARLOUR

ABBEY GREEN/
GREAT COURT

CELLARIUM
(STOREHOUSE)

CLOISTE

CELLARER'S
PARLOUR

Lay-brothers'
day stairs

CELLARER'S
OFFICE

KITCHEN

WEST
GUEST-
HOUSE

EAST
GUEST-
HOUSE

REFECTO

LAY-
BROTHERS'

REFECTORY

INFIRMARY BRIDGE

LAY-BROTHERS'

INFIRMARY

LAY-BROTHERS'

REREDORTER

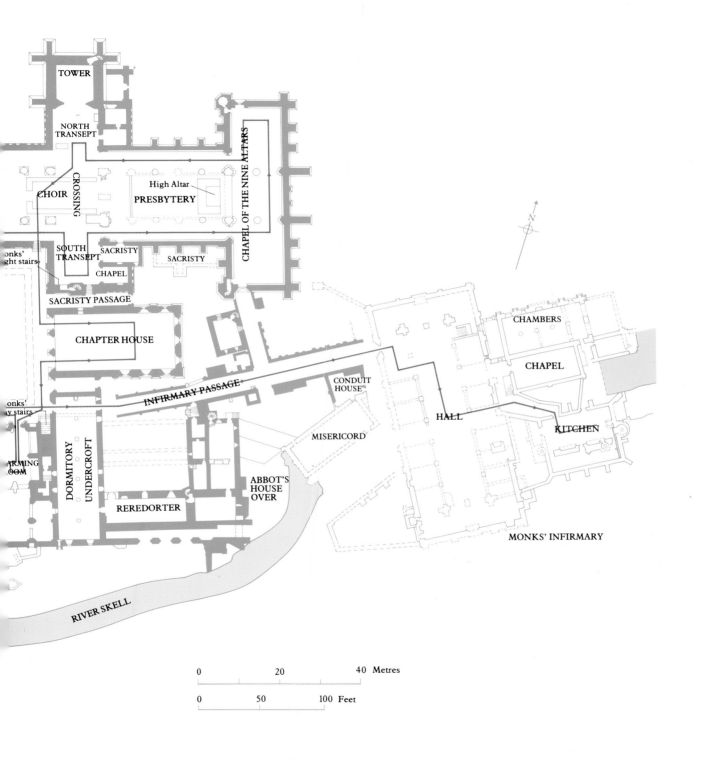

TOWER

NORTH
TRANSEPT

CHOIR

CROSSING

High Altar

PRESBYTERY

CHAPEL OF THE NINE ALTARS

SOUTH
TRANSEPT

SACRISTY

SACRISTY

onks'
ght stairs

CHAPEL

SACRISTY PASSAGE

CHAPTER HOUSE

INFIRMARY PASSAGE

CONDUIT
HOUSE

onks'
y stairs

CHAMBERS

CHAPEL

HALL

KITCHEN

MISERICORD

ARMING
OOM

DORMITORY
UNDERCROFT

ABBOT'S
HOUSE
OVER

REREDORTER

MONKS' INFIRMARY

RIVER SKELL

N

0   20   40 Metres

0   50   100 Feet

TOUR OF THE ABBEY

The main approach to Fountains Abbey is from the west, as it was in medieval times, along a narrow lane, once part of the outer court where charity was dispensed to the poor, the sick and travellers. It opens out into the great courtyard of the monastery; only fragments of the gatehouse are left. At this point, the path divides at the edge of abbey green and the view of the whole west range of Fountains across the wide expanse of lawn is unforgettable.

The right-hand path leads over the River Skell by way of a 14th-century bridge. Beyond, a wall crowns

All that remains of the narthex arcade that was once outside the west door of the church. Some of the abbey's benefactors were buried here.

the rising ground to the south of the monastic buildings, a section of the precinct wall that enclosed the 70-acre site. The left-hand path running past the abbey down the valley was constructed by William Aislabie in the 18th century as a carriageway for the use of visitors to Studley Royal.

THE ABBEY CHURCH

The tour begins at the west front of the abbey church, which faces the visitor across abbey green. This front was built about 1160 from sandstone hewn from the rock that outcrops along the north side of the valley beside the monastery. The stone weathers into a variety of subtle colours and Fountains has all the natural perfection of buildings that are superbly in harmony with their environment.

The first impression of the west front is of a flat, severe façade of Cistercian austerity in which the huge window appears disproportionately large. This great Perpendicular window was in fact inserted only in 1494, when Abbot John Darnton replaced the original rose window and the three round-headed openings underneath.

Go into the church through the doorway in the west end. The most remarkable feature of the building today is its scale, with a great uninterrupted vista from west to east framed by the massive Norman pillars of the nave on either side. But this is not how the church would have looked in the Middle Ages, when it was divided up by altars, chapels and screens. It was, in fact, two churches, accommodating the 'choir' monks at the east end and the lay brothers at the west. The cutaways at the bottom of the pillars of the nave once held

The great west doorway.

The south aisle of the church looking west.

the screens that shut off the lay brothers from the rest of the church. The north and south aisles were vaulted in stone, but the roof of the nave itself was of wood.

The walls of the nave show the simple restrained treatment of surfaces so typical of early Cistercian architecture. The windows in the clerestory, so-called because it enabled light to enter the church clearly and directly, are in the traditional, rounded form, a contrast with the more pointed arches of the nave. The manipulation of light was of outstanding importance in Cistercian interiors and the walls of the inside of the church would have been whitewashed.

Cross over to the south aisle, where there is a fine view down the length of the west range. Walk up the

The interior of the church was once covered with plaster, which was painted to simulate stonework.

One of the chapels in the south transept. This is the oldest part of the abbey and illustrates well the severe nature of Cistercian architecture.

aisle into the south transept. This is the site of the first wooden church built in 1133 and the oldest part of the abbey. It was through this transept that the monks entered the choir for night services, which began with Mattins about 2am, filing down the night stairs from the adjoining dormitory. The two transept chapels illustrate well the stern nature of Cistercian architecture. The inner chapel was altered in the 15th century, probably to make a sacristy; by then Fountains had accumulated such a wealth of treasures that their storage had become a problem. On the west wall of the transept can be seen some of the plaster that once covered the interior of the church, with a pattern of painted lines to simulate the stonework beneath.

Walk up to the east end, which is a complete contrast in style. The Early English presbytery and the Chapel of the Nine Altars belong to the early decades of the 13th century and were adorned with shafts of local Nidderdale marble. The high, pointed vaulting of the chapel caused structural problems and Abbot Darnton substituted a lower roof of wood in the reign of Henry VII. He also inserted the overpowering Perpendicular window in the centre of the east wall, which must have completely changed the Gothic character of the chapel. Fractures in the masonry appeared at the heads of two windows and these were concealed by curious bands of decorative sculpture; one in the last window on the left of the long east wall of the chapel has a scroll dated 1482 carried by an angel on the inside and the pagan symbol of a green man on the outside (perhaps symbolising the good within the church and the godless without).

Return down the church from the east end, past the site of the High Altar marked by a pavement of tiles. At

This carving of an angel holding three horseshoes is on an arch in the south transept.

The presbytery (*left*) was once ornamented with columns of dark Nidderdale marble (*right*).

26

When the impressive
Perpendicular window
was inserted in the
Chapel of the Nine
Altars, fractures appeared
at the heads of two
windows which were
concealed by bands of
decorative sculpture.
Here an angel adorns the
inside (*right*) while a
green man looks down on
the world outside (*above*).

(*Above*) Looking down the nave towards the great west window.

(*Right*) Floor tiles were used in the church from the early 13th century. This pavement marking the site of the high altar was assembled from those that survived in the time of William Aislabie.

28

the central crossing the monks sat in wooden stalls; earthenware acoustic jars placed underneath gave added resonance to their chanting. Look up at the Perpendicular tower built at the end of the north transept, constructed from local limestone and the work of Darnton's successor, Abbot Marmaduke Huby, in the reign of Henry VIII. It is 172 ft high and contains two spiral staircases, one in the north-east angle for the first two storeys, the other in the north-west corner giving access to the third or belfry storey and the battlements. The figure in the niche overlooking the abbey is possibly St Bernard. The inscriptions carved on the sides are taken from the Cistercian breviary or service book and all have the same theme: 'To the only God be honour and glory for ever', initialled M. H.

Steps lead into the cloister from a doorway in the south aisle. As the monks passed through, they would have crossed themselves with holy water from the stoup beside the door. The base of the stoup is still there and its fluted basin of Nidderdale marble was discovered during excavations in the abbey in the 1850s.

The cloister, showing the chapter house arcade.

THE CLOISTER

The cloister was the nerve centre of monastic life, a quadrangle protected on each side by covered arcades or alleys which communicated with every part of the abbey. The corners were set out as early as 1140, so the scale of the cloister must have been envisaged by then.

On the north side, against the wall of the church, the monks devoted themselves to the daily *lectio divina*, the slow process of contemplative reading involving meditation and especially prayer, designed for spiritual growth rather than intellectual exercise. Learning for its own sake was not encouraged and only novices received instruction and training, for there were no schools in Cistercian abbeys. Books for use in the cloister were kept in a cupboard in the wall of the south transept. Next to this cupboard lies a much smaller

The vaulting in the sacristy passage.

29

The chapter house is one of the few parts of the abbey with ornamentation. The corbels for the arches of the roof show a variety of carved decoration.

recess. This unusual survival was for a wax tablet in a frame on which the weekly duties of the monks were written.

The principal room in the east range of the cloister is the chapter house, so-called because a chapter of the Rule of St Benedict was read at the daily meeting. The chapter house was the administrative centre of the abbey, dealing with both religious and secular affairs. As time went on, the latter became increasingly important. The room was completed in time for Abbot Richard III to be buried there in 1170, the first of 19 abbatial burials at its east end. By the time the chapter house was completed the Cistercians had relaxed their insistence on unadorned architecture and some modest decoration was becoming acceptable. This is one of the few parts of the abbey ornamented with sculpture, with carved leaves and other simple designs on the corbels which once supported the stone vaults of the roof.

The monks' dormitory was overhead, where they took their six or seven hours rest a night. They would sleep girded in their habits and wearing their stockings, ready for the Lord's command, but their knives were laid aside for safety. Night slippers were put on before they filed down into the south transept for the night services, to pray for deliverance from the evils of darkness while the world slept.

The day stair to the dormitory rises from the south side of the cloister. This flight of steps also gives access to the muniment room where the abbey's documents were stored. This must have been regarded as particularly secure as King John kept some of the royal treasure in it; nine days after the signing of Magna Carta in June 1215 he ordered all the valuables and goods in the custody of Fountains to be dispatched secretly to him.

The south range of the cloister catered for the domestic side of monastic life. In the warming room beside the day stairs, wood fires burned from November until Easter, where the monks could warm themselves.

The room became a cold store for dairy produce when the emphasis of the abbey's economy changed from sheep to dairy farming in the 15th century and fires were no longer lit in the two enormous fireplaces. The 12th-century stonework in the warming room shows evidence of the use of eastern techniques. The dog-leg pattern in the archstones of the two fireplaces indicates that the mason concerned had some knowledge of Arab methods of stone-cutting, brought to Europe in the time of the Crusades.

The stone benches under arcading on either side of the refectory door in the centre of the range once supported lead-lined basins. Here the monks washed their hands before meals, drying them on towels from the cupboard in the outer wall of the warming house. Water was brought through lead pipes, examples of

The day stair to the monks' dormitory rising from the south side of the cloister. The arched recess on the right was a towel cupboard which the monks used when washing their hands before meals in the refectory.

which can be seen in the museum. This is one facet of the sophisticated system of water engineering at Fountains, in which the Cistercians excelled. The course of the Skell was diverted to the south to give space for building and from the dormitory a latrine block ran out east at right-angles to be flushed by the river. These 'necessaries' were called reredorters, literally 'rooms at the rear'.

The dignity and grace of the Early English architecture of the refectory are particularly fitting for a room the monks associated with the Last Supper. They sat on wooden benches round the walls and listened to works of a devotional nature being read from the pulpit on the west side while they ate. The stone supports for the tables still protrude from the grassy floor, the mark where the crucifix hung above the high table can still be made out, and a flight of steps in the wall leads up to the pulpit. The monks had two meals a day in summer but only one in winter. No meat was ever eaten in the refectory. It was provided for the elderly and sick in the infirmary, and when all monks were allowed to eat it on specified days from the early 14th century, it was cooked for them in the infirmary kitchen.

The food was brought in from the stone-vaulted kitchen next door to the refectory by means of a turntable hatch set in the connecting opening. The kitchen also served the lay brothers' refectory in the west range on the opposite side.

Great fires were lit in the warming room on 1 November every year and kept going until Easter.

The dog-leg pattern in the 12th-century archstones above the fireplaces in the warming room shows knowledge of Arab building techniques.

The refectory. The base of the pulpit is on the right. The wall between the two pairs of windows at the far end was adorned by a crucifix.

A doorway on the west side of the cloister leads into the cellarer's parlour of the west range. With a length of 300ft, the range runs from the church at one end over the river at the other. The northern end of the range linked the abbey with the outside world and was divided into cells. Beside the church, an outer parlour opened on to the great court. Here conversation was permitted in the interests of monastic business. Then came the cellarium (two storage areas) and the parlour for the cellarer, the monk in charge of domestic administration, with an entry into the cloister. His office or chequer projects outside the west range into the court. The rest of the range was occupied by the lay brothers' refectory.

Step outside into abbey green to see the projecting chequer. Above it the lay brothers' day stairs lead to their dormitory. This ran the entire length of the west range and could sleep 200 or more. Their night stairs descended into the south aisle of the church at one end. To the right as you face the west range is the north wall of the lay brothers' infirmary, with its three large windows. This is all that remains of the building that was constructed over the Skell on the south side of abbey green. The lay brothers' reredorter lies between the infirmary and the west range, and is best seen from the other side of the Skell (cross over the infirmary bridge).

The architecture of the west range shows how the

The scale pattern in white on the jamb of the doorway leading from the cloister into the cellarer's parlour is typical of the simplicity of early Cistercian decorative designs.

monks took care to preserve an outward appearance of regularity and unity when they extended the range to the south in the late 12th century. The pointed windows on the ground floor of the extension contrast noticeably with the windows in the older round-headed style to the left. However, all the windows at ground level would have been hidden behind a low wall that cut off the west range from the bustle and noise of the court. Only the upper windows would have been visible from abbey green and these are all in a unified round-headed style.

(*Above*) The lay brothers' reredorter, built over the River Skell.

(*Left*) The magnificent west range. The monks would not have enjoyed this uninterrupted view as the space was then partitioned.

(*Above right*) The east guest-house from abbey green. The circular window was blocked in the 14th century for the insertion of a flue.

(*Right*) The east guest-house, with the 12th-century infirmary bridge over the Skell in the foreground.

The two remaining guest-houses lie beyond the lay brothers' infirmary, to the east of the 13th-century bridge over the Skell. They have been much altered but originally each had two self-contained suites consisting of hall, chamber and privy, where important guests such as patrons and foreign wool merchants were lodged. The gable of the nearer, east guest-house has a circular window which was blocked in the 14th century for the insertion of a flue.

THE INFIRMARY

Return to the cloister and go out through the opening on the east side directly opposite the doorway to the west range. Pass through the undercroft of the monks' dormitory to emerge into the extensive infirmary complex, the most secluded part of the abbey. Ahead runs the infirmary passage. This was first built in wood which was later replaced with stone; the bases of the pillars can be seen on the left-hand side of the path. Nothing now remains of the timber galleries which were added above the passage, but a tall block of masonry on the right contains the back of a brick fireplace which would have heated an upper gallery.

Off to the right beside the river is the drainage

Refuse from the infirmary dropped through this grating into a channel of the Skell, the medieval equivalent of a waste-disposal unit.

(*Left*) An ornamented column in the east guest-house.

system of the monks' reredorter; this was probably more effective in the Middle Ages before the course of the Skell changed in places. Separate quarters were provided for the abbot on the east side of the reredorter site, but only a few traces survive. Abbot Huby rebuilt the accommodation as a Tudor house.

Little remains of the infirmary, but the re-erected pillars emphasise the distinction and scale of the great hall or infirmary ward, built in the Early English style at the same time as the Chapel of the Nine Altars and constructed on a platform over the river. The Skell flows underneath in four channels. The ruins between the hall and the abbot's house mark the area of the misericord (the dining-room where meat was eaten) and the conduit house which brought fresh, spring water to the abbey. The infirmary complex – hall, chambers, chapel and kitchens – is a second abbey in miniature, the product of wealth, engineering skill and monastic devotion to the needs of the sick and elderly. Illness might be regarded as the result of sin, but medical care was the most expert available. One homely relic is the grating over a channel of the Skell on the far side of the kitchen, a medieval waste-disposal unit through which the infirmary's refuse dropped into the river.

The re-erected pillars in the infirmary give some idea of the original scale and quality of building here.

STUDLEY ROYAL

'Ruins', said the 18th-century traveller Arthur Young, 'generally appear best at a distance.' The picturesque remains of Fountains Abbey lay just beyond the borders of the Studley Royal estate when John Aislabie started work on his landscaping scheme in the early 18th century. Initially the garden was planned without reference to the abbey, but the final layout included a spectacular view of the great Cistercian house as the culmination of a visitor's tour.

John Aislabie had inherited the Studley estate in 1693 through his mother's family. A socially and politically ambitious man, he was already Tory Member of Parliament for Ripon and by 1718, with the help of a timely change of political allegiance, he was Chancellor of the Exchequer in the new Whig administration. Work on the garden had started in the same year, at a time when Aislabie had, it seems, been considering running down the estate. His sudden decision to invest in forestry and land improvement, and to make a garden in the wildest part of the park, based on the wooded valley of the River Skell, was a major change in attitude towards Studley.

Then, in 1720, disaster struck. Aislabie was one of the principal sponsors of the South Sea Company scheme, the bill for which was promoted by him personally. After this vast financial operation collapsed in what became known as the South Sea Bubble, he was expelled from Parliament and disqualified from public office for life. Deeply embittered and disappointed, he returned to Yorkshire in 1721 and devoted himself to the creation of the garden, which he may have regarded as a refuge from public disgrace. In the same way, but inspired by very different motives, Cistercian monks had come to the valley five centuries earlier and founded the great abbey of Fountains as a retreat from the material world. After John Aislabie's death in 1742, his son William completed his father's scheme by purchasing the ruins of the abbey and designing the present approach to the imposing east front. He also extended the landscaped area in the picturesque romantic style which was then becoming fashionable and which contrasts directly with the formality of his father's work.

Between them, these two gifted amateurs created what is arguably the most important 18th-century water garden in England. Perhaps more remarkable, the

Early views of Fountains Abbey
and Studley Royal by Balthazar
Nebot, painted *c*.1760.
(*Above*) Tent Hill in the bite of
Half Moon Pond with the abbey
beyond; (*below*) the main cascade
into the lake from the water garden.
White swans as shown in this
painting have been reintroduced by
the National Trust

garden is still much as it was first conceived and as it was depicted in a series of early views attributed to the painter Balthazar Nebot. Perhaps because, on the death of William Aislabie in 1781, the estate passed to his daughter and then to her niece, the garden escaped major reshaping in a more romantic vein in the late 18th and early 19th centuries at a time when many other formal layouts were swept away in the pursuit of the 'natural' landscape.

The garden and park were subsequently preserved by later members of the Vyner family, descendants of the Aislabies, until both were purchased by West Riding County Council in 1966. The National Trust acquired the estate in 1983 and has embarked on a major scheme of restoration and conservation to restore Studley to its former glory.

Looking over the Moon Pond to the Temple of Piety, with one of the crescent ponds on the left.

DEVELOPMENT OF THE GARDEN

The water garden occupies about 60 of the 307 hectares (150 of the 760 acres) of the present estate. Its formal, geometric design was clearly inspired by the work of the great French landscape gardeners, such as Le Nôtre, but it is also entirely individual in character. Formal gardens of the period were invariably laid out with a dominant axis centred on the house, but at Studley the main axis was the river. In other respects, too, the scheme for Studley deviated from others of its date, for it was relatively small-scale, and never had the elaborate parterres that were such a feature of the French style. Instead, as a map or a bird's-eye view of the garden shows clearly (see pp. 48–49), the ponds and canal make a formal pattern of water in the centre of the valley.

Studley was also influenced by the work of Queen Anne's gardeners, George London and Henry Wise, who used elements of the French style but adapted them to English taste. Their designs were characterised by mirror-like stretches of water

The formal water garden with the Temple of Piety.

in which garden buildings and other features would appear reflected, set in lawns bordered by yew hedges and surrounded by plantations of forest trees. John Aislabie would have been able to learn from the garden of this kind laid out by his father-in-law, Edmund Waller, at Hall Barn in Buckinghamshire, and which Aislabie himself continued to develop after 1713. One of its features was the wide use of evergreen trees, which kept it green during the winter, and this policy was pursued again in the planting at Studley. Its importance lies partly in the fact that Studley is now the least altered survival of these 'green gardens' of early 18th-century England.

The garden makes ingenious use of the landscape. By his imaginative use of vistas and viewpoints, John Aislabie incorporated the two great medieval buildings – Fountains Abbey and Ripon Minster – which lay outside his estate, and used them to extend the boundaries of his own work. Unfortunately, none of the original drawings for the garden has survived, and there are few records of John Aislabie's thoughts and intentions at the time. The only professional advice he appears to

View down the canal from the rustic bridge, with the statue of Hercules and Antaeus on the left. The turf embankments beside the canal are part of John Aislabie's original design.

have received was from the distinguished Palladian architect, Colen Campbell, although he knew a number of other important architects and garden designers, including Roger Morris, whom he may have consulted. His gardener was an employee on the estate, William Fisher, while the garden works were carried out by local labour under the direction of another local man, John Simpson. Overworked and worn out by constant interference from Aislabie, Simpson's health broke down and he was succeeded by the master-mason Robert Doe from London in 1728.

The first phase of construction from 1716 to 1730 involved basic engineering and planting. Large-scale excavation works were needed to form the great semicircle with its geometric ponds, to canalise and dam the river for the main cascade into the lake and to level the valley floor. The Half Moon Pond was constructed as a reservoir for the canal at the point where it joined the river and the knoll known as Tent Hill in the 'bite' of the Moon was landscaped. The scale of the operation was enormous. Seven contractors were employed to bring stone from Galphay Moor some

A winter view of the cascade into the lake, with the rusticated columns and pavilions on the dam on either side.

four miles away, and a hundred men were taken on seasonally for the heavy manual work. In December 1720, the South Sea Bubble scandal brought work abruptly to a halt but it had resumed again by 1726. Progress was hindered by major changes of plan as work proceeded, principally involving the design of the main cascade into the lake. Simpson's accounts reveal that architectural problems were resolved by full-scale trial and error on site, a procedure which could only reflect the whims of his opinionated client. Small wonder that his health deteriorated!

Lawns were planted along the canal and around the ponds, bounded by yew hedges, turf embankments and ramps, and the garden was criss-crossed with formal walks and vistas. Trees were planted on the steeper slopes of the valley, beech and elm on the middle slopes, Scots pine near buildings and yew as underplanting.

The buildings and statuary were later additions to the design and only the pavilions known as fishing tabernacles at either end of the dam were completed by the time Simpson was forced to retire. Although the stables in the park had been started, building was suspended while Aislabie reconsidered the original design. Work seems to have gone more smoothly under Robert Doe's direction, perhaps because he was better able to handle his difficult employer. The buildings in the garden – the Banqueting House, the Octagon Tower, the Temple of Fame and the Temple of Piety – were constructed as 'eye-catchers' to complete the design, all being intended to highlight particular views across the valley.

The statuary seems to have been moved around the garden in the 1730s. With the exception of the statue of Hercules and Antaeus, it was all of lead, probably from the workshop of Andries Carpentière, the Flemish sculptor who worked in London – latterly under the name of Andrew Carpenter – and who also supplied figures for Powis in North Wales among other major houses. The lead figures of Bacchus and Galen were erected there in 1738, the same date as the Wrestlers replaced an earlier statue on the site below the Octagon Tower. It was originally set in the centre of a small fanshaped parterre, probably of coloured gravel and pebbles, but this was grassed over early this century. Four figures have disappeared: the Dying Gladiator from the edge of the canal opposite the Temple of Piety; Priapus from the woodland to the rear of the Banqueting House; Galen from the centre of the lower of the crescent ponds; and Pan from his position in the deer park, where he would have been visible from the Temple of Fame.

William, who succeeded to the estate in 1742, was less ambitious and flamboyant than his father. He too was MP for Ripon but, unlike his father, was content with relatively lowly office. His two major contributions to the garden were the purchase of the Fountains Abbey estate and the extension of the landscaping scheme below the lake, where the river flows down a narrow gorge beside the park. Here William took advantage of the rocky cliffs to create one of the first examples of the picturesque landscape style in England, a direct contrast to the ordered formality of the water garden. His work at Studley was followed by the creation of a similar garden at Hackfall on the River Ure, north-west of Ripon between 1749 and 1768. This was the period when the wild landscapes of the 'sublime' were very much in fashion. Where scenery was suitably untamed, naturally occurring features such as rocky outcrops were emphasised with buildings and trees to create an awesome effect of menace which was intended to strike terror into the hearts of visitors. This would be relieved by areas of the 'beautiful', in which controlled smoothness and the small-scale were predominant.

The steep valley of the lower Skell was an ideal subject for this treatment. The wildness of the natural landscape, with steep cliffs overhanging the river, was

The beech woods along the lower Skell were planted by William Aislabie to emphasise the dramatic nature of the valley

The structure known as the Devil's Chimney in the steep valley of the lower Skell, once decorated with four tall pinnacles.

accentuated by the eye-catchers William built on prominent outcrops, and by the beech woods he planted to tower over the valley and emphasise its vertical lines. Sadly, most of the garden features he constructed have disappeared. These included a Chinese pavilion, decorated with carved dragon heads and with little bells which tinkled harmoniously in the breeze, one of the first examples of *chinoiserie* in an English garden. William also built a feature known as the belvedere, which was probably one of several elegant late 18th- or early 19th-century summer-houses, none of which has survived. The only building to be seen in this section of the valley today is the curious structure known as the Devil's Chimney. Believed to have been inspired by a tomb near Rome, it has lost the four tall pinnacles which once decorated it.

William's purchase of the Fountains Abbey estate in 1767 was of much greater significance for Studley than his landscaping of the lower Skell. His father had tried to buy the property from the Messenger family for £4,000 as early as 1720 but had suddenly called the deal off and his neighbour had then refused to sell it.

M. J. Messenger's stubbornness on this point is said to have led Aislabie to obstruct his view over the garden by building up Tent Hill. Aislabie may also have realised he could enjoy the view of the abbey without going to the cost of buying it. William obviously thought otherwise and paid £18,000 for the 202-hectare (500-acre) estate, including the early 17th-century Fountains Hall and the remains of the great Cistercian house. In his landscaping of the approach to the abbey, William again broke away from the formality of his father's garden and created an informal sweep of grass along the Skell with woods on the valley sides providing a natural frame to the east end of the monastic church. He also engineered the surprise view of Fountains Abbey from the high path on the east side of the valley, one of the most memorable features of the garden today.

The surprise view of Fountains Abbey is best seen when the trees are without foliage.

PLAN OF THE ESTATE

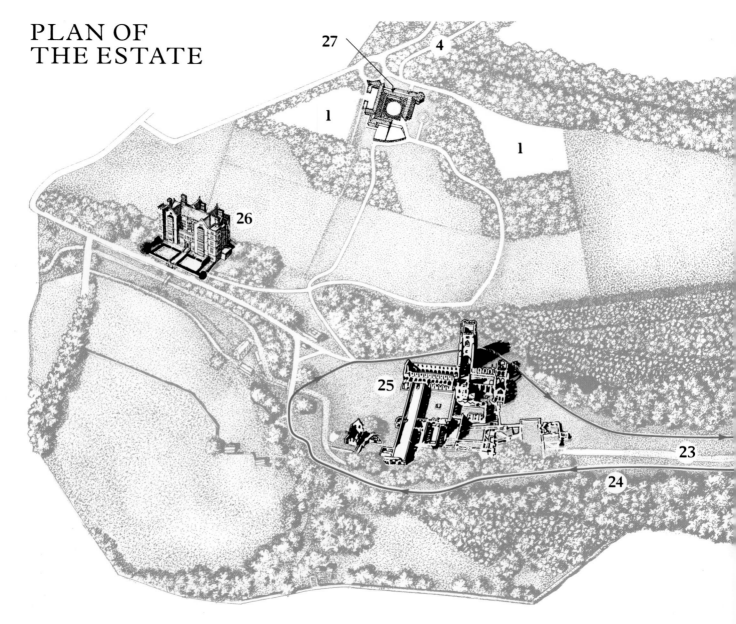

1 Car parks	**5** Deer park	**9** Canal	**13** Drum fall
2 Banqueting House	**6** Canal Gates entrance	**10** Moon Pond	**14** Rustic bridge
3 Lake	**7** Cascade	**11** Crescent ponds	**15** Quebec Monument
4 Footpaths to St Mary's Church	**8** Seven Bridges Walk	**12** Small Half Moon pond	**16** Temple of Piety

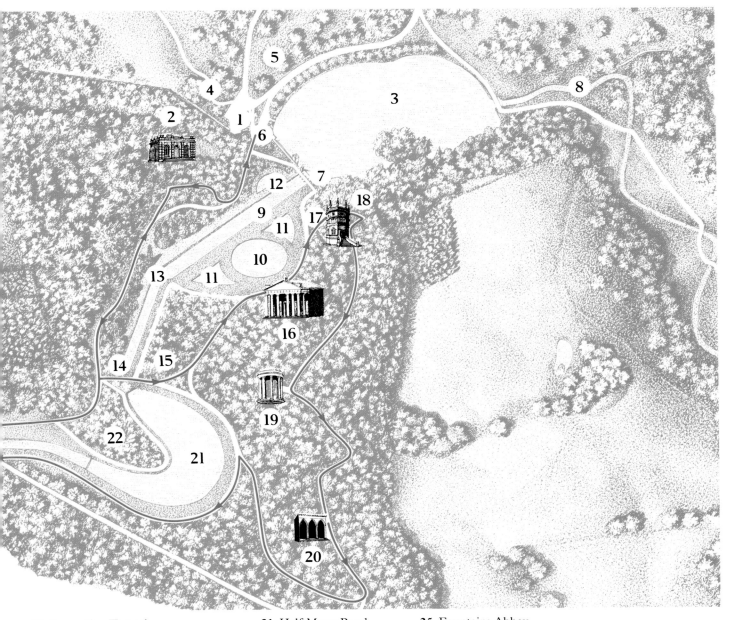

17 Serpentine Tunnel
18 Octagon Tower
19 Temple of Fame
20 Surprise view; Anne Boleyn's Seat

21 Half Moon Pond
22 Tent Hill
23 River Skell
24 Robin Hood's Well

25 Fountains Abbey
26 Fountains Hall
27 Visitor Centre

Route of walk

TOUR OF THE GARDEN

Although many visitors to Studley come into the gardens from Fountains Abbey, it is best to start a tour from the Canal Gates entrance, which is how the garden was designed to be seen. The building which is now a café at the Canal Gates was probably originally constructed as a house for the estate stewards of the 1st Marquess of Ripon in c.1860. But it was a tea-room by the 1890s, a reminder that Studley was as popular a century ago as it is now.

Follow the road along the canal with the water garden on the left, passing the Silver Pond on the right. The Octagon Tower is perched dramatically above the valley on the other side of the garden and the statue of the Wrestlers is just below the path. At the fork, follow the right-hand path between old beech trees to the Banqueting House. Seen across the coffin lawn, which would originally have been surrounded by a formally

Water lilies blooming on the small Half Moon pond.

clipped yew hedge, this delightful feature was built in c.1732 and was originally intended as an orangery. It was probably designed by Colen Campbell, who also had a hand in the architecture of the stables in the deer park, and has some fine wood carving inside by Richard Fisher of York.

The equestrian portrait of the Sultan of Surat over the fireplace is also original, but the furniture has been specially made. The elliptical tables with fake marble tops match the little columns on either side of the fireplace, while the 1760s-style wheelback chairs are exact copies of a set known to have been made for a garden building at Studley. There was once a small circular temple, not unlike the Temple of Fame, on the lawn in front of the Banqueting House, but this decayed and was demolished around 1775.

From the Banqueting House, the path descends to the right and returns to the road along the canal, with views over the yew hedges across the water garden. The rustic bridge was one of the original features in the garden. Look down to the left at the statue of Hercules and the giant Antaeus, the only one of stone in the garden (Antaeus was practically invincible because contact with the ground gave him renewed strength, but Hercules has managed to lift him up and is squeezing him to death).

Bear left over the bridge, past the curious feature known as the Quebec Monument. Why this place is associated with Quebec is no longer known, but a small cannon used to be fired here on 13 September every year to commemorate the anniversary of the capture of Quebec and the death of General Wolfe in 1759. The whole tangled area to the left of the path was originally a wilderness garden with a small lake. The

The Banqueting House was
probably designed by Colen
Campbell. The interior view
shows one of the apses with
wood carving by Richard
Fisher of York and high-quality
plasterwork.

origin of the Quebec Monument itself is not certain, but it is identical to the features which crown the balustrade over the dam and was probably made at the same time. On the right is the grotto, added to the garden at the same time as the rustic bridge, and a magnificent specimen of *Sequoia sempervirens* (coast redwood).

The path now curves round the semicircle of the water garden and this is the best place from which to appreciate its geometry and the placing of the statues. Neptune, the God of Water, has pride of place in the centre of the Moon Pond, with Galen and Bacchus on either side at the edge of the crescent

The rustic bridge. This was one of the original features and once marked the limit of the garden owned by John Aislabie

(*Left*) Hercules and Antaeus, the only stone statue in the garden

ponds. Backed by yews with Scots pine and beeches, the Classical building known as the Temple of Piety which overlooks the water garden from the path here was one of the last features which John Aislabie added to the garden after his health began to fail. It was designed as a cool garden house on the shady side of the valley. Originally dedicated to Hercules, whose labours could be compared with Aislabie's own achievements in the construction of the garden, it was renamed the Temple of Piety after new stucco decoration (of the Grecian daughter feeding her father) was created by Giuseppe Cortese in the late 1740s. The steep banks to the right of the path, as elsewhere in

Neptune has pride of place in the centre of the Moon Pond

(*Right*) Bacchus stands at the edge of one of the crescent ponds

the garden, have been replanted with the species of Aislabie's original scheme, including yew, box, guelder rose, juniper and sweet-briar.

At this point the short tour of the garden is concluded by continuing on along the path and crossing the bridge over the cascade back to the Canal Gates entrance. The longer route now bears right up the steep path below the Octagon Tower and very shortly plunges dramatically into a twisting tunnel. This feature, known as the Serpentine Tunnel, was cut through the hill and lined with stone in the mid-1730s as the garden began to expand at the top of the valley. It is much more impressive going up than coming down so those who tour the garden in the other direction do not get the full effect. On the right just before the tunnel you can see the remnants of the 18th-century footpath system.

Emerging at the top of the slope, the path now leads round to the right to the Octagon Tower on its high rocky outcrop. Constructed in the mid-1730s, it is a typical Gothick garden building, and a very early example of the use of this style. Today the views from the Octagon are inward – down onto the water garden and across the valley to the Banqueting House – but before the trees grew up there were superb views from the windows of the tower over Ripon Minster to the Cleveland Hills some 25 miles away.

The path now meanders along the top of the valley through beeches, yews and Scots pines, the elms that were once a feature of these woods having sadly

(*Above right*)
The Octagon Tower. Before the trees grew up, it was possible to see 25 miles to the Cleveland Hills from this point

(*Left*) The Temple of Piety with the statue of Neptune

far below in the valley, rising serenely from the banks of the River Skell. This is William Aislabie's surprise view, as impressive today as it was 200 years ago.

From here the path drops down to the right into the valley again to the edge of Half Moon Pond. Those who do not wish to continue to the abbey can now turn right and walk back through the water garden to the Canal Gates. The knoll on the other side of the pond, restored in 1997, is known as Tent Hill. It used to be crowned by another eye-catcher, an octagonal domed Temple of Venus. The route taking in the abbey bears left round the pond and up the romantically landscaped valley of the Skell. William Aislabie's 'natural' approach to the abbey here, the 'De Grey Walk', is a direct contrast to the formality of the water garden – the grass is longer, the edges less carefully trimmed. The view is framed by the woods on the valley sides,

A carpet of snowdrops in some of the fine woodland on the estate.

disappeared. The circular domed building (rotunda) known as the Temple of Fame is an architectural deceit; the sandstone columns are in fact constructed of hollow timber with a sanded finish to simulate stone. This is another good viewpoint, but the climax of the high path undoubtedly comes at the Gothic alcove known as Anne Boleyn's Seat, originally built in the late 18th century, but reconstructed several times since. Approached from behind, with trees crowding in on either side, there is no warning of what can be seen from inside the shelter. The abbey suddenly appears

William Aislabie was responsible for the informal sweep of grass leading up to the east end of Fountains Abbey

The lake below the dam. The island on the left is thought to be a 19th-century addition formed from lake dredgings

but unfortunately the passage of time and the ravages of Dutch elm disease have taken their toll and only a few of the older specimens remain. Both sides of the valley are being replanted to recreate William Aislabie's original scheme. The complete circuit of the garden is now concluded by returning to the Canal Gates entrance by the path on the opposite side of the valley, from which there is a good view down the canal to the dam.

For those who have time, it is also well worth circling the lake below the dam and following the path along the Skell where the river emerges on the other side. The route along the steep-sided valley here crosses from one side of the Skell to the other by delightful little

(*Left*) The Temple of Fame. The wooden columns have been restored to their original sanded finish, so as to simulate stone

The Seven Bridges Walk along the lower Skell zigzags from one side of the river to the other over delightful little arched bridges

Detail of the gate from the park into the water garden.

The East Gate, with the lime avenue climbing to St Mary's Church on the skyline.

arched bridges – which is why it is known as the Seven Bridges Walk. This is the valley that William Aislabie landscaped and remains of the paved fords which he built for visitors' carriages still lie alongside the bridges which carry the path.

THE DEER PARK, STABLES, FORMER HOUSE AND CHURCH

The original entrance to the Studley estate was through East Gate, from the estate village of Studley Roger. Here there is an arched carriage entrance with square-arched pedestrian gates and lodges on either side added in the 18th century. From the gate, a majestic avenue of lime trees climbs slowly to the skyline and St Mary's Church, a High Victorian Gothic building built by William Burges in 1871–78. On either side is the 161-hectare (400-acre) deer park, still grazed today by a substantial herd of about 350 deer, mostly fallow deer with smaller numbers of Red and Manchurian Sika. The park is the oldest feature of the Studley estate and was already well established when John Aislabie came into his inheritance. It is also the only part of the estate where Aislabie's layout has not survived, with only slight traces remaining of the seven great intersecting avenues which Aislabie designed to focus on features of the estate, on Marmaduke Huby's tower or on a distant view of Ripon Minster. During the late 18th and early 19th centuries the park was gradually made less formal in line with the fashion of the time and the influence of Lancelot (Capability) Brown and others. Today, the gently undulating ground is a splendid place for a walk or a picnic, the rough pasture dotted with magnificent specimens of forest trees, notably oaks, beeches, limes and sweet chestnuts. Some gnarled and twisted specimens pre-date the Aislabies.

The deer park once enclosed Studley Royal House

The stables in the park, all that remains of Studley Royal House. These are now privately owned.

The magnificent park is grazed by a substantial herd of deer.

Some of the trees in the park are gnarled and twisted with age.

St Mary's Church, William Burges's religious masterpiece

wards. Only the impressive stable block has survived, built between 1728–32 in the newly fashionable Palladian style and again attributed to Campbell. The main feature of the stables is its massive open-arched loggia facing eastwards over the deer park, but the building is privately owned and is not open to visitors.

The Anglican church of St Mary the Virgin was the fourth eye-catcher to be built at the end of the long avenue. The first was a stone pyramid, based on the one at Stowe intended as a monument to John Aislabie. This was replaced by a wooden obelisk, in turn supplanted in stone by 1815. This survives just west of the church but the latter was a visual focus of a different

The winged Lion of Judah which supports a shaft on the south side of the sanctuary

(*Right*) The sanctuary roof over the altar in St Mary's Church is a vision of heaven with angels playing musical instruments

but this too has not survived. The medieval manor house, which John Aislabie inherited, was damaged by fire in 1716, rekindling his interest in Studley. It is one of the great mysteries of the estate that he never rebuilt a great house here. When William inherited the estate from his father he made extensive improvements to the house, most notably, commissioning plans from Daniel Garrett and plasterwork from Giuseppe Cortese. Initially a Gothick creation, the façade of the house was changed to a more traditional classical style in the 1760s. Sadly, this building too was extensively damaged by fire in 1946 and was demolished shortly after-